Tujague's Cookbook

Creole Recipes and Lore in the New Orleans Grand Tradition

Poppy Tooker

PELICAN PUBLISHING COMPANY

Gretna 2015

The word "Pelican" and the depiction of a pelican are trademarks of Pelican Publishing Company, Inc., and are registered in the U.S. Patent and Trademark Office.

Library of Congress Cataloging-in-Publication Data

Tooker, Poppy.
  Tujague's cookbook : Creole recipes and lore in the New Orleans grand tradition / Poppy Tooker.
     pages cm
  Includes index.
   ISBN 978-1-4556-2038-8 (hardcover : alk. paper) — ISBN 978-1-4556-2039-5 (e-book)
  1. Cooking, American—Louisiana style. 2. Cooking, Creole—Louisiana style. 3. Tujague's (Restaurant) I. Title.
   TX715.2.L68T644 2015
   641.59763—dc23
                        2015013031

Chapter-divider photographs by Sam Hanna

Printed in China

Published by Pelican Publishing Company, Inc.
1000 Burmaster Street, Gretna, Louisiana 70053

Mark, Braden, and Candace Latter (Photograph by Sam Hanna)

in the mirrors lining the walls. Crystal chandeliers were hung in the large upstairs dining room, which was named the Krewe d'Etat Room for a popular satirical, relatively new Carnival krewe with a unique style that pokes fun at the old-line krewes.

Krewe d'Etat is ruled by a "Dictator" instead of a traditional, crowned monarch. The membership of this irreverent organization is allegedly made up of members from old-line Carnival krewes such as Comus and Momus that ceased parading in the early 1990s.

The room is decorated with lighted cases displaying ball favors and other memorabilia, and the fireplace is tiled in mosaics proudly proclaiming *Krewe d'Etat*. Krewe members gather in the space for annual luncheons and other special occasions.

For over a century, Tujague's diners simply ate a traditional table d'hôte meal; nothing else was offered. The five-course menu always began with shrimp remoulade, followed by beef brisket, then soup or salad. Entrées changed each day, with Steven allowing diners a choice of fish or meat. Dessert was usually bread pudding, but occasionally pecan pie or cheesecake would make an appearance. When Mark took the helm, he introduced new menu items and, radically, à la carte items. Diners could now order whatever they wanted from the menu and craft their own meals.

Though the dining room has a fresh look and the menu has evolved, the historic bar remains largely unchanged. Tourists and regulars still stand elbow to elbow along its broad expanse, enjoying camaraderie and cocktails as they have since 1856.

(Photograph by Sam Hanna)

Tujague's Spirited Ghosts

It is inevitable that the second-oldest restaurant in America's most haunted city could lay claim to ghosts of its own. Who are the spirits at Tujague's?

During his tenure at Tujague's, Steven Latter said that while sitting alone in his usual corner of the bar, every morning at the same time the door of the downstairs ladies' room would loudly slam shut. Upon investigation, there was never anyone there.

After Steven's death, sous chef Jamie Byrd was in the second-floor men's room when he heard the adjacent ladies'-room door slam. At the time, he was the only person in the building. For the rest of that day he could not get the electric Robot Coupe food processor to turn on, although other kitchen employees could. Jamie also said that every time someone would send him to the third floor, all the hairs on his arms would raise on end. Eventually, he simply refused to go back there.

Jamie wasn't alone in his fear of Tujague's third floor. Yet another party had a brush with something unexplainable at Tujague's, this time in the early weeks of 2015. After a spirited dinner, emboldened by many bottles of wine, a group of eight gentlemen asked manager Victor Dinh if they could tour the upstairs rooms. "Sure," he said. "Have a look at anything you'd like." The group embarked on a self-guided tour.

A few weeks later, one of the gentlemen returned, asking for Victor. "Listen," the man implored, "I owe you an apology."

"For what?" Victor asked. "Your group was very generous."

"You don't understand," the man said, clearly embarrassed. "You have to accept my apology. When we were here recently and you said we could look around, we went up to the third floor and I stole a framed photograph I found up there."

"No worries," Victor assured him. "We don't keep anything of value in the attic."

"Please accept my apology," the man begged. "You see, from the moment I stole that photograph, terrible things have happened. Immediately that night, I lost my wallet, keys, and cellphone. My best friend has had a stroke and is in the hospital, and my wife was in a car accident."

It is assumed that the spirits of Tujague's Restaurant wanted to ensure that all of the archival images stored on the third floor would be available for use in documenting their history in this book.

The door leading out to the street from today's rear dining room was the original entrance to Madame Bégué's restaurant. The only other entrance was through the bar, an area where honorable ladies of the late nineteenth and early twentieth centuries would never have been seen. Steven Latter christened that dining room the Bégué Room and lined the walls with photographs from the period. Of particular note is an aged, sepia-tinted image of an elegantly attired woman of the early 1900s. She stares beguilingly at the camera, a suggestive smile on her lips.

Steven Latter relished having his picture taken with movie stars and notable figures

NBC News journalist John Chancellor, Steven Latter, and Miriam Latter
(Tujague's Private Collection)

when they drank and dined at Tujague's. His collection of framed photos, many of them autographed, adorned the walls in every room of the restaurant and bar.

It turns out that displaying celebrity photographs at Tujague's was a tradition that began with Hipolyte Bégué. Julian Eltinge, a celebrated cross-dressing actor of the early 1900s whose given name was William Julian Dalton, was a star of both stage and screen. Julian was able to transform himself into such a beautiful woman that Dorothy Parker wrote:

> My heart is simply melting at the thought of Julian Eltinge;
> His alter ego, Vesta Tilley, too.
> Since our language is so dexterous,
> Let us call them ambi-sexterous—
> Why hasn't this occurred before to you?

Julian was paired with silent-movie star Rudolph Valentino in the film *Isle of Love*. In 1910, *Variety* magazine called him "as great a performer as there is today." Seven years later, he performed in New Orleans and, of course, dined at Bégué's. Julian was befriended by Hipolyte Bégué and signed two photographs for him as mementoes of his visit.

At the time of Steven Latter's death, one of Julian Eltinge's photos hung in the Bégué Room. When Mark Latter undertook some much-needed restorations in 2013, Julian's photos and many more were warehoused in the third-floor attic. This clearly disturbed the Tujague's ghosts.

That autumn, Ian Wrin and his fiancée, April Russ, visitors from Falling Waters, West Virginia, enjoyed dinner in the Bégué Room. Ian snapped a self-portrait of the two of them with his camera. Upon returning home, they downloaded the photo and discovered a ghostly image in the back corner of the room, hovering over another table of diners.

Chapter 1

Cocktails from America's Oldest Standup Bar

Tujague's bar of the early twentieth century (Tujague's Private Collection)

It's little wonder that the oldest standup bar in America is in the city where the cocktail was created. Elizabeth Kettenring Dutrey opened Dutrey's Coffee Exchange with her husband, Louis, in 1867. "Coffee exchange" was the pleasant name given to barrooms in those days, although what most patrons were imbibing was a lot more spirited than coffee. An imposing mirror backs the bar. The piece is said to have spent nearly a century in a Parisian bistro before it was shipped to New Orleans. Imagine the passing parade of history reflected in *that* mirror!

Two years after Louis's death, Hipolyte Bégué became Madame's barkeep—then her husband—and the tradition continued.

In 1914 the bar became "Tujague's" and ownership passed to Philip Guichet and John Castet. Four years later, Philip travelled to New York City to compete in a national cocktail contest. His creation, the frothy, mint-hued Grasshopper cocktail, placed second. Upon Philip's return to the corner of Madison and Decatur, the Grasshopper became a patron favorite and remains such.

Even Prohibition could not alter the tradition of Tujague's bar. "Yeah—we tried to close for a few hours when Prohibition began, but it just didn't work out," Philip Guichet said of the era. Photos of that time are particularly revealing. The once liquor-laden bar is devoid of vessels. A soda syphon and bottles of near beer—a brew containing less than one-half of 1 percent alcohol—are all that remain on display. Gentlemen stand innocently at the bar wearing an expression that says, "Nothing's going on in here." In truth, the liquor never stopped flowing. Waiters spiked drinks from bottles concealed in their apron pockets.

In 1931, Tujague's made headlines. The *New Orleans Times-Picayune* reported: "New Orleanian Philip Guichet was seized by a raider after serving absinthe. He denied selling liquor despite the accusations of a Prohibition agent who claimed to have seen him serving absinthe to a patron in the restaurant below his apartment."

Once Prohibition ended, Philip continued to compete in national cocktail competitions. In 1956, he travelled to New York City for the Early Times National Mixed-Drink Competition. He vigorously shook together whiskey, cream, orange flower water, sugar, an egg, and ice. Finished with a sprinkle of nutmeg, the cocktail was served in a stemmed glass. The drink Philip called Whiskey Punch won first place.

At home, life in the bar at Tujague's was good. Philip devoted his life to it and was amply rewarded. He poured bourbon for Harry Truman and made a Sazerac for Dwight Eisenhower. For Philip, Tujague's was a family affair, and his sons, Otis and Philip, Jr., grew up in the business and spent much of their lives working the bar. Politicians, judges, prizefighters, and movie stars all flocked to Tujague's, where it was never too early for a drink.

The center of the action in the bar was a big, square table. Otis's earliest memories were of his father sitting there with friends, eating beef brisket with horseradish sauce, breaking fresh cap-bread loaves, and swapping tall tales.

In the family tradition, Otis's son, Ronald "Noonie" Guichet, was working as a Tujague's busboy by the time he was sixteen. He has fond memories of the activity at that barroom table, where everyday regulars would sit from lunchtime on, rolling poker dice. When Steven Latter purchased Tujague's from the Guichet heirs in 1982, Noonie stayed on as bar manager.

It is an obscure fact that, in a state renowned for lax liquor laws, the sale of miniature bottles was prohibited in Louisiana until 2014. Steven Latter was fascinated by the miniatures and collected them. Customers brought him rare and unique minis from their global travels and he displayed these gifts in glass cases throughout the restaurant and bar. The collection numbers in the thousands and visitors still marvel at them today.

Steven in his favorite spot at Tujague's
(Photograph by Louis Sahuc)

Mark remembers that his dad rarely drank alcohol, but when he did, his drink of choice was Crown Royal. A few years before his death, Steven saw a Crown Royal throne that he simply had to have. He pestered Michael Shlenker of Glazer's, one of Louisiana's largest liquor distributors, to secure one for him. Once his purple velvet throne was installed in the back corner, from its cushy comfort Steven held court in America's oldest standup bar.

(Photograph by Sam Hanna)

(Photograph by Sam Hanna)

Grasshopper

In 1918, on the eve of Prohibition, Philip Guichet travelled to New York City to participate in a prestigious cocktail contest. His creation—the Grasshopper—placed second in the competition, but it has remained a winner at Tujague's bar ever since.

Makes 1 cocktail

¾ oz. green crème de menthe
¾ oz. crème de cacao
¾ oz. white crème de menthe
½ oz. brandy
¾ oz. heavy cream
¾ oz. whole milk
½ tsp. brandy for topper

Combine all ingredients, except for the brandy, in a cocktail shaker filled with ice. Shake vigorously. Strain into a champagne flute and top with brandy.

Early Times National Mixed-Drink Competition, 1956 (Tujague's Private Collection)

Pimm's Cup

The refreshing Pimm's Cup was created in London in 1840. Traditionally Pimm's liqueur was combined with lemonade, a dash of soda water, and a cucumber garnish. Tujague's takes the Pimm's Cup to new heights with a proprietary base crafted in-house. Fresh fruits and vegetables are macerated for three weeks with Pimm's liqueur. The fruits and vegetables are strained off and the enhanced liqueur goes back into the bottle for mixing to order in the customary way.
Makes 1 cocktail

1½ oz. Pimm's base (recipe follows)
½ oz. simple syrup (recipe follows)
½ oz. freshly squeezed lemon juice
½ oz. freshly squeezed lime juice
Club soda
1 thin slice cucumber

Pour Pimm's base in a highball glass filled with ice. Add the simple syrup and lemon and lime juices; stir. Top with club soda. Garnish with a slice of cucumber.

Pimm's Base

Makes 1 fifth

1 celery heart with leaves, finely chopped
¼ cup each finely chopped strawberries, blueberries, and raspberries
1 medium cucumber, chopped
Half a lemon
Half a lime
Half an orange
1 fifth Pimm's liqueur

Combine all ingredients, crushing solids to extract juices. Macerate together in a sealed container set in the refrigerator for 3 weeks. Strain. Store in a cleaned liqueur bottle in the refrigerator.

Simple Syrup

Makes 1 cup

1 cup sugar
1 cup water

Combine sugar and water in a saucepan and cook over a medium heat until it reaches a boil. Cook until the sugar has dissolved, 1-2 minutes. Remove from heat and cool to room temperature. Store in a clean glass jar with a lid. Syrup can be refrigerated for up to 6 months.

(Photograph by Sam Hanna)

Old Fashioned

Noonie Guichet remembers batching large quantities of Old Fashioneds early on Sunday mornings. The whiskey-laden drinks were stacked up on the back of the bar in anticipation of the post-Mass rush. As soon as High Mass at St. Louis Cathedral concluded, those thirsty Catholics stormed the bar at Tujague's for the first drink of the day!

Makes 1 cocktail

1 sugar cube
Half an orange slice
1 maraschino cherry
2 dashes Angostura bitters
2 dashes Peychaud bitters
Splash simple syrup (see index)
2 oz. bourbon whiskey

Muddle sugar cube, orange, cherry, bitters, and simple syrup in an old fashioned glass. Fill glass with ice, then top with bourbon.

(Photograph by Sam Hanna)

Zesty House Bloody Mary

This breakfast cocktail's name comes from a legend of divination. Believers stand before a mirror and call out Bloody Mary's name three times, expecting an apparition who will reveal the future. Have enough of these spicy drinks and who knows what you can conjure.

Makes 1 cocktail

1½ oz. vodka
½ oz. freshly squeezed lemon juice
½ oz. freshly squeezed lime juice
Bloody Mary base (recipe follows)
Pickled vegetables for garnish, such as green beans,
    peppers, cucumbers, tomatoes, or okra (optional)

Pour the vodka and lemon and lime juices in a highball glass filled with ice. Fill the glass with Bloody Mary base. Stir to combine. Garnish with pickled vegetables if desired.

Bloody Mary Base

Makes about 6 ½ cups

46 oz. tomato juice
2 tbsp. ground black pepper
½ cup Crystal hot sauce
½ cup olive juice
½ cup Lea & Perrin's Worcestershire sauce
1½ oz. prepared horseradish

Combine all ingredients.

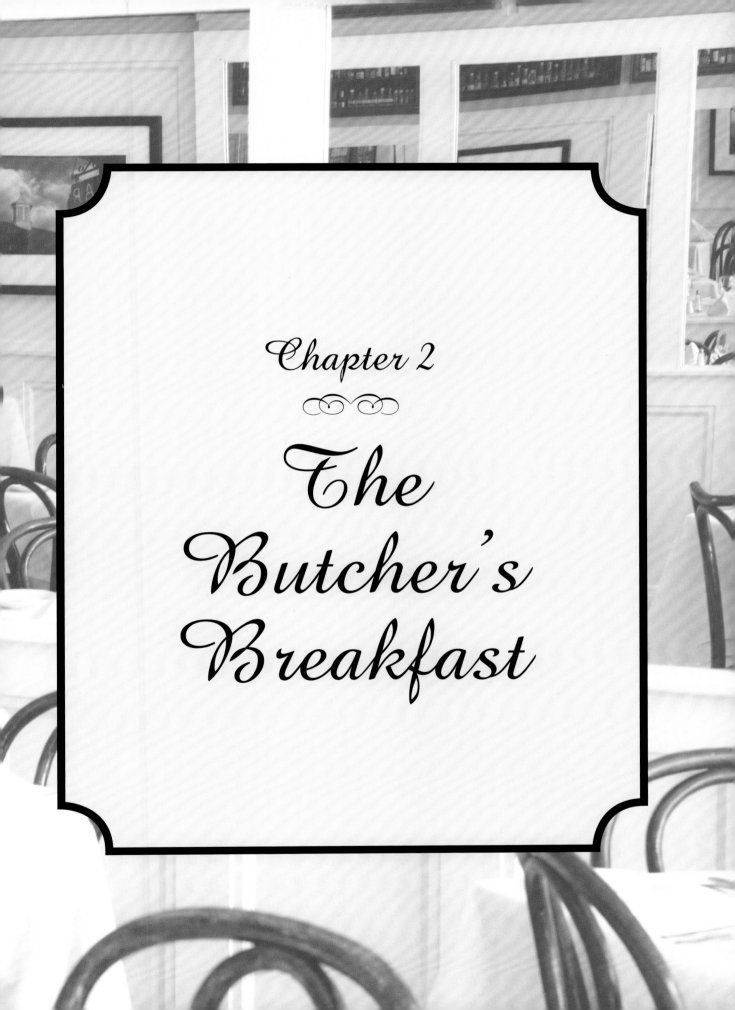

Chapter 2

The Butcher's Breakfast

German born, Elizabeth Kettenring Dutrey Bégué arrived in New Orleans in 1854 to join her brother, who worked as a butcher at the French Market. Shortly thereafter, she met and married Louis Dutreuil, one of her brother's fellow butchers. His American patrons claimed not to be able to pronounce Dutreuil, so by 1867, when Louis and Elizabeth established a business across Decatur Street from the butcher's market, it was called Dutrey's Coffee Exchange. At that time, a "coffee exchange" was actually a barroom where coffee was also served.

Elizabeth noticed how hungry her brother and his fellow butchers were every midday. Their workdays began in the predawn hours, fueled only by coffee and a croissant. Hence, Elizabeth established the tradition of serving a hearty meal for the butchers every morning at eleven o'clock. The seven-course breakfast varied daily according to what was available at the bustling French Market just across the street. Standard on the menu were eggs accompanied by an additional four courses, washed down with generous amounts of wine and chicory-laced coffee.

Elizabeth's dining room only accommodated thirty guests. For the first decade or so, her patrons were mostly butchers. Hence, the meal we regard today as brunch was originally known as the "butcher's breakfast."

When Louis Dutrey died, Elizabeth ran the bar and restaurant alone for two years. One day she crossed the street to the butcher's market and met handsome, dapper Hipolyte Bégué, a man eight years her junior. Knowing a good thing when she saw it, Elizabeth offered him the position of barkeep. Hipolyte followed her back across the street and they married soon after. Dutrey's Coffee Exchange became Bégué's Exchange.

A Sunday-morning breakfast at Bégué's (The Historic New Orleans Collection, acc. no. 1974.25.29.20)

By the time the Cotton Exposition (the precursor of the World's Fair) opened on the site of today's Audubon Park in 1884, Bégué's had become the city's premier tourist attraction. American travellers poured into the city by train, hoping to experience the famed "breakfast at Bégué's," and Hipolyte charmed guests as he presided over the dining room with a grand flourish. But still, there were only thirty seats in the restaurant, where one fixed menu was served just once every day, precisely at 11:00 A.M. The tourists crowded out the butchers, and business boomed as never before.

After Elizabeth Bégué died in 1906, the widowed Hipolyte quickly married her young kitchen assistant, Françoise Laforgue Laporte. In doing so, he magically created a second "Madame" who seamlessly carried on the dining tradition. But in 1916, Bégué's abandoned its original location and moved across the street to the uptown corner of Decatur and Madison.

In turn, Tujague's moved from its original location, a few doors down Decatur, to the original Bégué's site. Tujague's was already serving a version of the butcher's breakfast but had never achieved the fame of Bégué's. Once they moved to the original Bégué's location on Decatur Street, Tujague's was in the spotlight.

Breakfast was eventually replaced by lunch and dinner service. In the 1980s, Steven Latter renovated the upstairs rooms where Madame had served her famous meals and reintroduced brunch to Tujague's patrons.

Madame Bégué in her kitchen (The Historic New Orleans Collection, acc. no. 1974.25.29.24)

Oysters Benedict

Eggs Benedict is a commonplace brunch dish, but succulent fried oysters from the Gulf of Mexico set this version apart from the rest.

Serves 6

6 Tujague's Buttermilk Biscuits (recipe follows)
Classic Hollandaise Sauce (see index)
Vegetable oil for frying
3 dozen large Gulf oysters, shucked
2 cups corn flour seasoned with Creole seasoning to taste
12 3-inch pieces tasso, baked ham, or Canadian bacon
¼ cup butter, softened

While the biscuits are baking, make the Hollandaise Sauce and set aside in a warm place.

Using a deep fryer or Dutch oven, heat the oil to 350 degrees.

Dredge the oysters in the seasoned corn flour, shake to remove excess flour, and fry until they float to the surface and turn golden brown, about 3-4 minutes. Do not overcook. Remove with a slotted spoon and drain on a platter lined with paper towels. Keep warm.

Heat the tasso, ham, or Canadian bacon in a skillet over medium-high heat, turning after about 2 minutes.

Split the biscuits in half widthwise. Spread each side generously with softened butter.

For each portion, place 2 buttered biscuit halves on a serving plate. Top each biscuit half with 1 piece tasso, ham, or Canadian bacon and 3 fried oysters. Drizzle each portion generously with Hollandaise Sauce.

Tujague's Buttermilk Biscuits

Makes 1 dozen

4 cups all-purpose flour
½ cup sugar
¼ cup baking powder
¾ cup (1½ sticks) salted butter, chilled
2 cups whole milk or buttermilk

Preheat oven to 350 degrees.

In a large bowl, combine the flour, sugar, and baking powder. Work in the cold butter until just combined. Add enough milk to form stiff dough; you may not end up using the full 2 cups.

Roll out the dough and cut circles using a 2½- to 3-inch cookie cutter or rocks glass.

Place the biscuits on greased baking sheet and bake until golden, about 15-20 minutes.

Breakfast Shrimp and Grits

Although New Orleans breakfast menus have long included a dish of breakfast shrimp, Charleston, South Carolina lays claim to Shrimp and Grits, a relative new addition to New Orleans' menus.

Serves 6

1 red bell pepper
Creole Shrimp Sauce (recipe follows)
BBQ Onions (recipe follows)
3 lb. Gulf shrimp, peeled and deveined, tails intact
Creamy Stone-Ground Grits (see index)
Hot French bread

Set the broiler on high heat. Broil the bell pepper directly under the broiler until skin blisters, about 5 minutes. With tongs, rotate pepper a quarter-turn. Broil and rotate until all sides are blistered and blackened. Immediately place pepper in a large bowl; cover and let stand for 20 minutes. Peel off and discard the charred skin. Remove the stem and seeds. Finely chop the bell pepper. Set aside.

Add the Creole Shrimp Sauce to a large skillet set over medium-high heat. Cook until simmering. Add the reserved red pepper and the BBQ Onions, and cook until heated through. Add the shrimp and cook, stirring, until the shrimp are thoroughly pink, about 5 minutes. Serve with Creamy Stone-Ground Grits and hot French bread.

Creole Shrimp Sauce

Makes about $3^1/_3$ cups

2 tbsp. vegetable oil
½ cup minced garlic
1 cup Lea & Perrin's Worcestershire sauce
½ cup lemon juice
2 cups Abita Amber beer
¼ cup Crystal hot sauce
½ cup dried rosemary
Salt and pepper
2 cups heavy cream

Add the oil to a large skillet set over medium-high heat. Sauté the garlic until fragrant, about 1 minute. Add the Worcestershire sauce, lemon juice, beer, hot sauce, rosemary, salt, and pepper to taste. Bring to a boil. Reduce heat to medium low and simmer until syrupy, about 30 minutes. Strain and return to skillet. Add the heavy cream and heat but do not boil.

BBQ Onions

Utilizing the flavor profile of BBQ shrimp, this unusual onion preparation adds a bit of that BBQ flair to all sorts of dishes. Red onions give the garnish great eye appeal.

Makes about ¹/₂ cup

1 tbsp. vegetable oil
1 large red onion, julienned
2 tbsp. Crystal hot sauce
2 tbsp. Lea & Perrin's Worcestershire sauce
Creole seasoning

Add the oil to a skillet set over medium-high heat. Add the onions and cook until translucent and soft, about 4 minutes. Add the hot sauce and the Worcestershire sauce. Stir. Cook until all liquid has evaporated, about 5 minutes. Add Creole seasoning to taste.

(Photograph by Sam Hanna)

(Photograph by Sam Hanna)

Bananas Foster Pain Perdu

Perhaps the most famous flaming dessert in the world is Bananas Foster, invented in 1951 by Chef Paul Blange at Brennan's Restaurant. When combined with pain perdu *("lost bread"), it becomes a luscious brunch dish.*

Serves 6

3 cups milk
½ cup sugar
4 tbsp. brandy
¼ tsp. nutmeg
½ tsp. cinnamon
12 thick slices stale French bread
1 stick butter
8 eggs, beaten
Powdered sugar
Bananas Foster Sauce (recipe follows)
Vanilla ice cream (optional)

Mix together milk, sugar, brandy, nutmeg, and cinnamon. Dip each piece of bread in milk mixture, allowing to absorb enough liquid to moisten but not fall apart. Drain and reserve.

Melt butter in a skillet over medium-high heat. Dip each piece of bread in the beaten eggs. Working in batches if necessary, slide the coated bread slices into the frying pan and cook until golden, about 2-3 minutes per side. Serve with a dusting of powdered sugar, Bananas Foster Sauce, and ice cream if desired.

Bananas Foster Sauce

Serves 6

¼ cup dark rum
5 tbsp. butter
1 cup brown sugar
¾ tsp. cinnamon
¼ cup banana liqueur
6 bananas, peeled and cut on a diagonal

Pre-measure the rum into a measuring cup and reserve.

Melt the butter in a flambé pan or 10-inch skillet set over medium heat. Reduce the heat to low and stir in the brown sugar. Cook, stirring continuously until the sugar is dissolved, about 5 minutes. Add ½ tsp. cinnamon and the banana liqueur. Working in batches if necessary, lay the banana slices down in the pan. Cook the bananas until they begin to soften and brown. Carefully turn them to caramelize the other side.

Pour the rum into the pan and tilt the pan slightly to ignite the rum. While the rum is flaming, toss in the remaining cinnamon by the pinch for added pyrotechnical effect. This is optional.

Creole Cream Cheese Pie

Today, many New Orleans restaurants offer Creole Cream Cheese Cake for dessert. Madame Bégué once again displayed her culinary prowess by transforming our native, soft cheese—normally served at breakfast—into this rich dessert.

Serves 6 to 8

2 9-inch piecrusts, uncooked
1¾ cups Creole Cream Cheese (recipe follows)
2 eggs
½ cup sugar

Preheat the oven to 350 degrees.

Line a pie plate with 1 piecrust. Cut the other into ¹/₂-inch strips and reserve.

Beat together the Creole Cream Cheese, eggs, and sugar. Pour the mixture into the pie plate. Adorn the top with the reserved crust strips woven into a lattice design.

Bake until pie is set and top is golden, 35-40 minutes. Cool to room temperature before serving.

Creole Cream Cheese

The original indigenous cheese of South Louisiana, Creole cream cheese is a soft, single-curd variety similar to France's fromage blanc. *French Creoles traditionally made it with day-old clabbering milk, hung it in cheesecloth in the shade of oak trees, then enjoyed it with a little cream and sugar for breakfast. The German dairy farmers, first to commercially produce Creole cream cheese in the early 1800s, preferred to eat it savory style, seasoned with salt and black pepper. By the time Madame Bégué transformed it into a dessert pie, Creole cream cheese was readily available across the street from her restaurant at the French Market. After nearly becoming extinct in the late twentieth century, today Creole cream cheese is again sold at farmers' markets and groceries across South Louisiana. It's also quite easy to make at home.*

Makes about 4 pt.

2 qt. skim milk
½ cup buttermilk
Pinch of salt
5 drops liquid vegetable rennet (available in health-food stores)

Combine all ingredients in a large stainless or glass bowl. Cover lightly with plastic wrap and leave out on kitchen counter at room temperature for 18-24 hours.

You will find 1 large curd cheese floating in whey. Use a slotted spoon to transfer the solid curd into 4 pint-sized cheese molds (or make your own by poking holes in plastic pint containers with a soldering iron).

Put the molds on a rack in a roasting pan and again cover lightly with plastic wrap. Refrigerate and allow to drain for 6-8 hours before turning over the molds. Store the cheeses in tightly covered containers for up to 2 weeks.

(Photograph by Sam Hanna)

Oysters à la Governor Noe

Steven Latter had been the proprietor for only four years when he had the opportunity to celebrate a significant Tujague's anniversary. To commemorate their 130th year, he asked the fêted bon vivant Christopher Blake to create a special baked oyster dish to be served for the first time on November 14, 1986. Oysters à la Governor Noe was named for James A. Noe, Louisiana's forty-third governor, who served a brief three-and-a-half-month term in 1936 following the death of Gov. Oscar K. Allen. His family members were regular diners at Tujague's and one of the upstairs private dining rooms was known as the Noe Room.

Serves 6

Rock salt
3 dozen large, cleaned oyster shell halves
1½ cups liquid (combine oyster liquid with white wine)
3 dozen large Gulf oysters
2 tbsp. butter
¼ cup finely chopped green onions
1 tbsp. finely chopped parsley
Salt
1 tsp. Tabasco sauce
2 tbsp. flour
6 thin slices country sausage (not breakfast sausage),
   fried

Preheat the oven to 350 degrees.

Spread thick layers of rock salt across the bottoms of several large jellyroll pans. Nestle the oyster shells, cupped sides up, into the rock salt so the shells are stable.

Add the liquid to a large sauté pan set over medium-high heat. When the liquid simmers, add the oysters and poach just until they plump and the edges curl. Remove oysters and retain 1¼ cups liquid. Add a bit more white wine if necessary. Set aside and keep hot.

Melt the butter in a sauté pan set over medium-high heat. Add the green onions and the parsley, and sauté until the onions are translucent, about 2 minutes. Add salt to taste and the Tabasco sauce. Stir in the flour, blending to make a light roux. Slowly add reserved hot liquid, whisking constantly until the mixture is thick and smooth.

Place 1 slice of country sausage and 1 poached oyster in each oyster shell. Divide the sauce evenly among the oysters. Bake the oysters for about 15 minutes until hot and bubbly.

Serve 6 oysters per person.

Seared Jumbo Lump Crab Cakes with Roasted Pepper Salad

Commonly served along the Eastern seaboard, crab cakes roared into popularity in late-twentieth-century New Orleans. Steen's, an old Louisiana company most famous for their thick, sweet, cane syrup, introduced a cane vinegar to the market at about the same time. Cane vinaigrette adds piquancy to sweet, roasted peppers, providing a perfect foil to luscious lump crab.

Serves 6

5 tbsp. unsalted butter, divided
½ medium red onion, finely chopped
¼ cup each finely chopped red and green bell peppers
1 garlic clove, minced
¼ cup finely chopped fresh parsley
Creole seasoning
1 lb. jumbo lump Gulf crabmeat, picked over
3 tbsp. mayonnaise
1 egg, lightly beaten
4 saltine crackers, crushed
1¼ cups plain breadcrumbs, divided
Vegetable oil for pan frying
Roasted Pepper Salad (recipe follows)
Sauce Ravigote (see index)

Melt 3 tbsp. of the butter in a large sauté pan over high heat. Add the onion, bell peppers, and garlic and cook until vegetables are fragrant and translucent, about 4 minutes. Add the parsley and the Creole seasoning to taste. Remove from heat and gently fold in the crabmeat, taking care not to break up the lumps.

Scrape the mixture into a large bowl and allow to cool. Add the mayonnaise and the egg, then add the crushed crackers and ³/₄ cup breadcrumbs, mixing thoroughly yet gently.

Shaped the crab mixture into 12 2-inch patties. Gently coat the patties with the remaining ¹/₂ cup breadcrumbs. Chill for at least 2 hours.

Heat the remaining butter and the oil in a large skillet set over medium-high heat. Working in batches, fry the crab cakes until golden brown, about 4-5 minutes per side, adding more oil if necessary. Drain on paper towels.

Serve 2 crab cakes per person atop a bed of the Roasted Pepper Salad. Drizzle with Sauce Ravigote.

Roasted Pepper Salad

Serves 6

2 large yellow bell peppers
2 large red bell peppers
BBQ Onions (see index)
Cane Vinaigrette (see index)
2 tbsp. finely chopped fresh parsley
1 garlic clove, minced
½ tsp. garlic powder
Creole seasoning

Set broiler on high.

Broil the peppers directly under the heat source until skins blister, about 5 minutes. With tongs, rotate peppers a quarter-turn. Broil and rotate until all sides are blistered and blackened. Immediately place peppers in a large bowl; cover and let stand for 20 minutes.

Peel off and discard the charred skins. Remove the stems and seeds. Cut the peppers into thin strips; place in a large bowl. Add the BBQ Onions and stir to combine. Set aside.

In a small bowl, whisk together the Cane Vinaigrette, parsley, garlic, garlic powder, and Creole seasoning to taste. Pour over the pepper and onion mixture and toss to coat. Cover and refrigerate for up to 4 hours.

Allow the salad to come to room temperature before serving.

(Photograph by Sam Hanna)

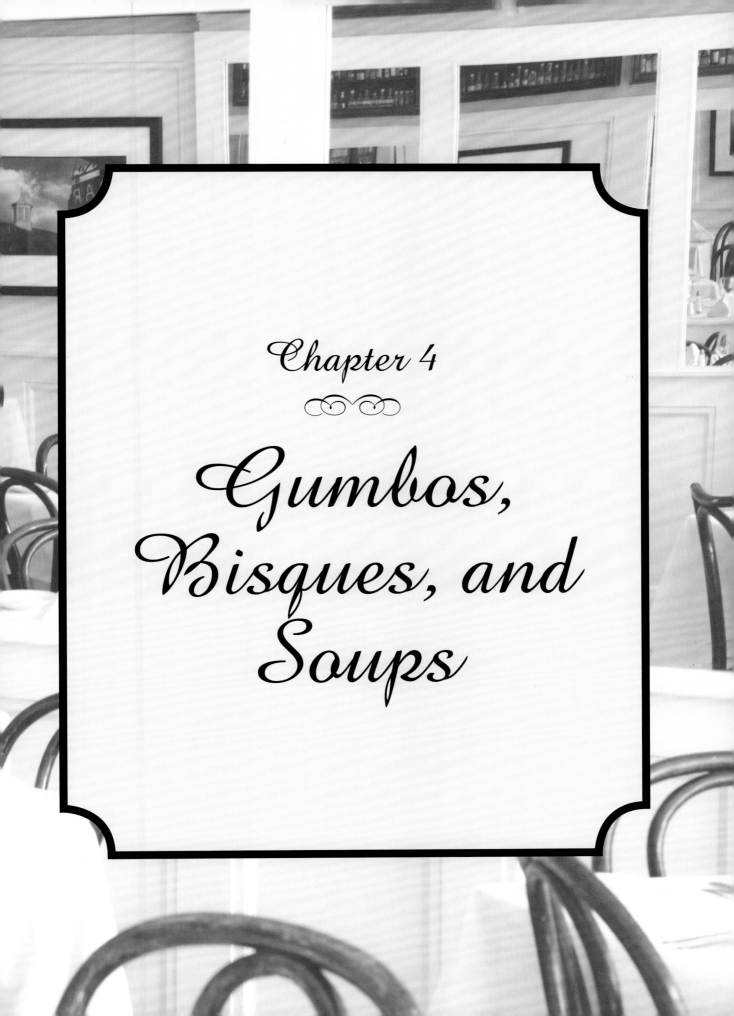

Chapter 4

Gumbos, Bisques, and Soups

(Photograph by Sam Hanna)

Since Tujague's earliest days, every table d'hôte meal included a course of soup or gumbo. Each Madame Bégué was renowned for her soup preparations, which were so rich they could be served as a meal.

Photographer Louis Sahuc turned soup into a personal ritual at Tujague's. For many years, he and several friends lunched there every Wednesday, in part because the vegetable beef soup was always served on that day.

One Wednesday, Louis had a hankering for mashed potatoes. He knew that they were served on Fridays with the fish entrée, but he asked Steven Latter if there might be some available on Wednesday. That day, Louis was served his usual bowl of vegetable beef soup with a side of mashed potatoes. He spooned the potatoes right into the soup and that became his favorite Wednesday lunch. Soon, everyone at Louis's lunch table was enjoying the unusual combination.

Louis recalled that one day, a small boy dining at an adjacent table with his mother was intently watching the grown men eagerly spooning mashed potatoes into their soup. Louis smiled at the boy and said, "At Tujague's, there's no rules about eating. We just eat what we like!"

Vegetable Beef Soup

The boiling liquid, beef, and vegetables from Tujague's Boiled Brisket of Beef make a most delicious base for vegetable beef soup. This soup has remained a Tujague's tradition since the days of Madame Bégué, who advised, "Hint to housewives: Do not throw away the vegetables, and save the stock. If you wish, cook vermicelli in the liquid and serve a fine, wholesome, delicious soup."

Serves 10 to 12

1 tsp. olive oil
1 tsp. water
½ lb. okra, sliced into rounds
4 qt. skimmed and strained stock reserved from
    Madame Castet's Boiled Brisket of Beef (see index)
    or store-bought beef broth
4 tbsp. tomato paste
1 cup dried red kidney beans
1 large onion, peeled and cut in chunks
4 bay leaves
2 large Russet potatoes, peeled and cut in chunks
3 large carrots, peeled and cut in chunks
2 ribs celery, cut in chunks
½ small head cabbage, cut in chunks
2 cups fresh or frozen corn kernels
2 cups fresh or frozen green peas
Beef and vegetables reserved from Madame Castet's
    Boiled Brisket of Beef, if available
Salt and pepper

Preheat the oven to 425 degrees. Whisk together the olive oil and water and toss the okra in the mixture. Place the okra on a baking sheet in a single layer. Set a timer and stir the roasting okra every 5 minutes, each time resetting the timer for another 5 minutes, for a total of 15. The okra will be slightly browned and wrinkled.

Meanwhile, heat the stock to boiling in a soup pot. Add the tomato paste and whisk until thoroughly incorporated. Add the red beans, onion, and bay leaves, and boil until the beans begin to soften, about 30 minutes. Add the potatoes, carrots, celery, and cabbage. Return to a boil, reduce heat to medium, and cook until potatoes and carrots are softened, about 15 minutes. Reduce the heat to medium low. Add the corn, peas, okra, and any leftover beef and vegetables from making Boiled Brisket of Beef, if available. Cook until heated through, about 10 minutes. Season with salt and pepper to taste.

Crawfish Bisque à la Bégué

This highly labor intensive dish is a rarity on today's New Orleans menus. Boiled crawfish are readily available in season and now crawfish tail meat can be purchased in one-pound bags. Occasionally, cleaned crawfish heads are also available in local groceries. Twenty-first-century crawfish bisque is still a time-consuming project, but it's worth it.

Serves 8 to 10

3 lb. boiled crawfish in their shells
12 cups water
1 cup + 2 tbsp. butter, divided
2 onions, chopped, divided
1 cup cubed fresh French bread
2 lb. crawfish tail meat, divided
Salt and black and cayenne pepper
1½ cups flour, divided
8 green onions, finely chopped
4 tbsp. finely chopped parsley
1½ tsp. thyme
2 bay leaves
Hot cooked rice

Peel boiled crawfish and reserve all parts separately (meat, shells, and heads).

Thoroughly wash all crawfish heads and reserve.

Take crawfish shells and make a stock by combining them in a stockpot with the water and all parings from the seasoning vegetables used in the bisque. Bring to a boil and simmer together for 10-15 minutes. Strain and reserve the stock.

Melt 4 tbsp. butter in a skillet. Add ¹/₂ cup chopped onion and sauté until lightly browned.

Soak French bread in as much water as it will absorb. Mince 1¹/₂ cups crawfish tails, then combine with the browned onions and the moist French bread. Mix together well and season with salt and peppers.

Stuff each crawfish head with filling, then roll in 1 cup flour. Melt 6 tbsp. butter in a skillet and brown stuffed crawfish heads. Reserve.

In a 5-qt. Dutch oven, melt ¹/₂ cup butter. Make a roux by whisking in ¹/₂ cup flour, cooking together until caramel colored. Add 1¹/₂ cups chopped onion and cook till translucent. Whisk in the stock. Add the green onions, parsley, thyme, bay leaves, and salt and peppers. Bring to a boil, then reduce to low heat and simmer together for 30 minutes. Fifteen minutes before serving, add remaining crawfish tail meat and stuffed crawfish heads, and simmer over low heat. Serve over cooked rice.

Crab and Spinach Bisque

The addition of bright green spinach to this creamy, crab soup makes this bisque as beautiful as it is delicious.

Serves 10 to 12

4 10-oz. bags fresh spinach, rinsed several times and
    dried
1 lb. (4 sticks) butter
⅓ cup flour
½ cup Shrimp Stock (see index)
4 cups heavy cream
12 oz. cream cheese, at room temperature
8 cups whole milk
1 lb. jumbo lump Gulf crabmeat, picked over
Salt and white pepper

Finely chop the spinach and set aside.

Melt the butter in a large pot or Dutch oven over medium heat. Add the flour and whisk until fully incorporated. Immediately add the Shrimp Stock and blend thoroughly. Add the cream and the spinach, and blend thoroughly. Reduce the heat to a low simmer. Do not boil.

Add the cream cheese to a separate saucepan over medium heat. When the cream cheese is melted, whisk in the milk. When the mixture is heated through and smooth, add to the spinach mixture in the other pot, whisking thoroughly. Gently fold in the crabmeat, taking care not to break up the lumps. Simmer the bisque until heated through, about 5 minutes. Season to taste with salt and white pepper.

Chapter 5

The Madame's Main Course

(Photograph by Sam Hanna)

Miss Brenda's Red Beans and Rice

In New Orleans, Mondays have always been the day reserved for red beans and rice. They are available seven days a week at Tujague's, but on Monday evenings, everyone who orders a drink at the bar gets a complimentary plate of red beans and rice served with smoked sausage and a piece of Miss Brenda's cornbread.

Serves 6 to 8

1 lb. dried red beans
2 sticks butter, divided
2 cups finely chopped onions
2 tbsp. minced garlic
2 cups finely chopped celery
2 cups finely chopped bell pepper
1 lb. smoked sausage, cut into 2½-inch pieces
4 smoked ham hocks
Hot cooked rice
Miss Brenda's Cornbread (recipe follows)

Cover the red beans with water and soak overnight.

Melt 1 stick butter in a 7-qt. saucepot over medium heat. Add the onion and garlic and sauté until the onions are translucent, about 5 minutes. Add the celery, bell pepper, and sausage and cook until the vegetables are tender and the fat has rendered from the sausage, about 10 minutes.

Drain the red beans and add to the pot with the ham hocks. Cover with water and bring to a simmer. Cook until the beans are soft, about 2¹/₂ hours, stirring often to make the beans creamy.

Remove the ham hocks, cut the meat from the bones, and add the meat back into the pot. Discard the bones. Stir in the remaining butter. Serve over hot cooked rice with Miss Brenda's Cornbread on the side.

Red Beans on Monday at Tujague's bar
(Photograph by Sam Hanna)

Miss Brenda's Cornbread

Miss Brenda's cornbread is so sweet and light, it could almost double as dessert. Served alongside the Monday red beans and rice, it completes the meal nicely.

Serves 6

6 tbsp. unsalted butter, melted, plus butter for baking dish
1 cup cornmeal
¾ cup all-purpose flour
1 tbsp. sugar
1½ tsp. baking powder
½ tsp. baking soda
¼ tsp. salt
2 large eggs, lightly beaten
1½ cups buttermilk

Preheat the oven to 425 degrees. Lightly grease an 8-inch baking dish.

In a large bowl, mix together the cornmeal, flour, sugar, baking powder, baking soda, and salt.

In a separate bowl, mix together the eggs, buttermilk, and butter. Pour the buttermilk mixture into the cornmeal mixture and fold together until there are no dry spots (the batter will still be lumpy). Pour the batter into the prepared baking dish.

Bake until the top is golden brown and a tester inserted into the middle of the cornbread comes out clean, about 20-25 minutes. Cool for 10 minutes before serving.

Madame Castet's Boiled Brisket of Beef

Boiled brisket of beef is a classic butcher's meal. Hungry butchers from the French Market, just across Decatur Street from Tujague's, expected to be served a course of long-simmered brisket, a plentiful, inexpensive cut of beef, as part of their meal. The special Creole touch is in the cold, spicy red sauce, heavily spiked with horseradish and fiery, coarse-ground Creole mustard. Creole mustard was first made commercially by Emile Zatarain and was a staple in Creole kitchens by the late nineteenth century.

Mme. Bégué's Recipes of Old New Orleans Creole Cookery, originally published in 1900, underwent small changes with each reprinting. At some point, Clemence Castet, the Madame of the Tujague's dining room from 1914 until her death in 1969, was persuaded to add their famous Boiled Brisket of Beef to the recipe collection. It appeared in the 1937 edition.

The first Madame Bégué advised in her 1900 cookbook, "If your beef brisket is not of the tender variety you may have to let it cook a little longer—deft prodding with a fork will inform you when it is ready to satisfy the inner man."

Serves 6 to 8

4 lb. beef brisket, trimmed
1 gal. water
¼ cup salt
12 black peppercorns
3 bay leaves
2 ribs celery, chopped
2 turnips, peeled and quartered
2 carrots, peeled and sliced
2 onions, sliced
½ small head cabbage, chopped
2 leeks, thoroughly washed, sliced (white and pale-green parts)
2 large tomatoes, preferably Creole, quartered
Creole mustard
Horseradish Sauce (recipe follows)

Place the brisket and water in a very large Dutch oven or deep soup pot, and add the salt, peppercorns, and bay leaves. Bring to a boil over high heat.

Add the celery, turnips, carrots, onions, cabbage, leeks, and tomatoes. Let the pot return to a boil, then reduce to a simmer and cook until the beef is tender, about 2½ hours. As it cooks, skim the surface of the water frequently to remove any scum that may accumulate.

Remove the brisket and reserve the cooking liquid and vegetables for other uses. Serve the brisket with Creole mustard and Horseradish Sauce.

Horseradish Sauce

This sauce also doubles as a cocktail sauce for cold, boiled shrimp and crab.

Makes 2 cups

½ cup creamed horseradish
½ cup Creole mustard
1 cup ketchup
Couple of dashes of Worcestershire sauce

Combine all ingredients. Chill the mixture for 6-8 hours or overnight to marry the flavors.

(Photograph by Sam Hanna)

Chicken Bonne Femme

The literal translation of bonne femme *is "good woman" but it usually is meant as "good wife." Any good French housewife would have this simple dish in her repertoire. This garlicky favorite has been an off-menu special request at Tujague's since it was introduced by Mme. Clemence Castet.*

Serves 4 to 6

1 fryer chicken, cut into 10 pieces (have your butcher
    cut the breasts in half)
Salt, pepper, and granulated garlic
Vegetable oil for frying
2 large Idaho potatoes, unpeeled and cut into ⅛-inch-
    thick slices, preferably on a mandoline
Persillade (recipe follows)

Dry the chicken thoroughly, then season liberally with salt, pepper, and granulated garlic.

Add 2¹/₂ inches oil to a large, heavy skillet, preferably cast iron. Heat the oil until smoking. Carefully add the chicken pieces. Just as the chicken begins to color, add the potatoes and cook until both the chicken and the potatoes are golden, about 15 minutes, turning and moving as necessary. Using a slotted spoon, remove the chicken and the potatoes from the oil and drain on paper towels. Season the potatoes with salt and pepper.

Immediately arrange the chicken and potatoes on a platter and sprinkle the Persillade generously on top.

Persillade

Persil is French for parsley. The finely chopped combination of this green, leafy herb and garlic known as persillade *is the most important ingredient in Tujague's repertoire, where it doesn't just crown the bonne femme but also finds its way into vegetable dishes, sauces, and stuffings. Once you begin to experiment with it, you'll always have a jar at the ready in the refrigerator.*

Makes about 1 cup

1 large bunch flat-leaf parsley, leaves only (no stems)
3 heads (about 40 cloves) fresh garlic, peeled

Place the parsley and the garlic in a food processor. Using the pulse button, chop the mixture until fully blended but do not puree. Cover well and store in the refrigerator for up to 5 days.

(Photograph by Sam Hanna)

(Photograph by Sam Hanna)

(Photograph by Sam Hanna)

(Photograph by Sam Hanna)

Brined Double-Cut Pork Chops with Abita Root Beer Glaze

The Abita Brewing Company is nestled in the piney woods just across Lake Pontchartrain from New Orleans. Since the brewery's earliest days in 1986, they've enjoyed a very special relationship with Tujague's. At one time, they even made a private-label beer just for the restaurant. Their sweet root beer makes a perfect glaze for chicken or pork. Don't skip the brining process. That's how you're guaranteed to have the juiciest pork chops.

Serves 6

6 cups water
½ cup kosher salt
½ cup packed light brown sugar
½ cup Crystal hot sauce
1 cup ice cubes
6 12-oz. double-cut bone-in pork chops
Vegetable oil
Abita Root Beer Glaze (recipe follows)

In a large pot, bring the water to a boil. Remove from heat and add the salt, brown sugar, and hot sauce, stirring until salt and sugar are dissolved. Add the ice cubes and chill until cold. Place the pork chops in the brine and set a plate on top to keep meat completely submerged. Cover with plastic wrap and chill overnight.

Remove chops from brine and pat dry.

Brush an outdoor grill or stovetop grill pan lightly with vegetable oil. Cook the pork chops, working in batches if necessary, until they register 145 degrees, about 5 minutes per side.

Preheat the oven to 400 degrees.

Transfer the chops to an ovenproof dish or, if using a grill pan, simply proceed to brush both sides of the chops with the Abita Root Beer Glaze. Place the dish or grill pan in the oven and cook until the surfaces of the chops are caramelized, turning halfway through, about 2 minutes per side. Chops will be medium.

Abita Root Beer Glaze

Makes about 2 cups

12 oz. Abita Root Beer
1½ cups light corn syrup
Salt and pepper to taste

Combine all ingredients in a small saucepan set over medium-low heat. Cook until syrupy, about 15 minutes. Cool.

Filet Tujague's with Fried Oysters and Crystal Hot Sauce Béarnaise

Since 1923, the Baumer family has manufactured Crystal Pure Hot Sauce in Louisiana. With a less intense heat than other pepper sauces, Crystal allows the pepper flavor to shine through without making a dish overwhelmingly spicy. The element of vinegar makes it a perfect choice for accenting the Béarnaise that sauces the filets and fried oysters in this contemporary presentation.

Serves 6

Crystal Hot Sauce Béarnaise (recipe follows)
6 8- to 10-oz. center-cut beef filets
¼ cup olive oil
Salt and freshly cracked black pepper
Vegetable oil for frying
1 dozen large Louisiana oysters
1 cup yellow corn flour, seasoned with Creole
    seasoning

Make the Crystal Hot Sauce Béarnaise and keep warm.

Preheat a gas, charcoal, or electric grill or stovetop grill pan.

Brush the filets with the olive oil and season with salt and pepper to taste. Place the filets on the grill and cook to desired doneness, about 4 minutes per side for medium rare. Set the filets aside, loosely tent with foil, and allow to rest for 10 minutes.

Using a deep fryer or Dutch oven, heat the oil to 350 degrees.

Dredge the oysters in the seasoned corn flour, shake to remove excess flour, and fry until they float to the surface and turn golden brown, about 3-4 minutes. Do not overcook. Remove with a slotted spoon and drain on a platter lined with paper towels.

For each portion, form a base at the center of each plate with ¹/₂ cup Crystal Hot Sauce Béarnaise. Plate a filet atop each. Evenly divide the fried oysters among the filets and drizzle on more Crystal Hot Sauce Béarnaise. Serve at once.

Crystal Hot Sauce Béarnaise

Makes 3 cups

¼ cup cane vinegar
2 tbsp. dried tarragon leaves
1 tbsp. finely chopped shallots
6 egg yolks
1½ lb. butter, chilled
½ tsp. salt
1 tsp. fresh lemon juice
1 tsp. Crystal hot sauce

Place the vinegar, tarragon leaves, and shallots in a small pan over medium heat. Cook for 5 minutes until all of the liquid has cooked out of the pan, leaving the tarragon leaves and shallots still moist. Set aside.

In a double boiler set over medium heat, combine the egg yolks with the cold butter, salt, and lemon juice. Whisk the ingredients continuously until the mixture has increased in volume and achieved a consistency that coats the whisk. If the sauce appears too thick, add a few drops of cold water to achieve the proper consistency.

Whisk the reserved tarragon reduction and the Crystal hot sauce into the sauce base.

(Photograph by Sam Hanna)

Chicken and Sausage Jambalaya

The name "jambalaya" is said to come from the French word for ham, jambon; *the word for rice in the African Bantu dialect,* ya; *and the French* à la, *meaning "prepared with the ingredient of." Jambalayas are as various as gumbos in Louisiana. Everyone has a different version. The jambalaya served at Tujague's today includes smoked sausage instead of ham and is brown in color, like the jambalayas of Cajun country.*

Serves 10 to 12

1 lb. smoked sausage, sliced
1 lb. boneless, skinless chicken thighs, cut into bite-
    sized pieces
2 cups chopped onions
1 tbsp. minced garlic
2 tsp. dried thyme
4 cups long-grain white rice, uncooked
8 cups hot Chicken Stock (see index)
Salt and pepper

Preheat the oven to 350 degrees.

Add the sausage to a very large Dutch oven, preferably cast iron, set over high heat.

When the fat begins to render from the sausage, add the chicken and stir. When the fat begins to render from the chicken, add the onion and cook until the onion is translucent, about 6 minutes. Add the garlic, thyme, and rice, and stir until the rice is thoroughly coated in the rendered fat.

Add the hot Chicken Stock and bring to a boil. Cover.

Place the Dutch oven in the hot oven and bake until the rice has absorbed all of the stock, about 25 minutes. Season with salt and pepper to taste.

Crawfish Étouffée

Crawfish étouffée is a smothered stew. The name originates from the French culinary verb étouffer, *meaning to simmer in a covered pot with natural pan juices. Crawfish, shrimp, or chicken cooked in this manner are all referred to as étouffée. The springtime arrival of mudbugs, as crawfish are called, at the French Market was always a cause for celebration. Seasonally, crawfish étouffée was included in the Tujague's table d'hôte meal.*

Serves 6 to 8

¼ cup vegetable oil
¼ cup all-purpose flour
2 cups chopped onion
1 cup chopped celery
½ cup chopped green bell pepper
2 tsp. minced garlic
2 bay leaves
2 cups Shrimp Stock (see index)
2 lb. domestic crawfish tail meat with fat
Salt and cayenne pepper
2 tbsp. unsalted butter
2 tbsp. chopped parsley
2 tbsp. chopped green onions
Hot cooked rice
Minced parsley for garnish

(Photograph by Sam Hanna)

Heat the oil until shimmering in a heavy skillet set over medium-high heat. Add the flour and cook, stirring constantly with a wooden spoon, until a dark roux is achieved, about 10 minutes. Add the onion and cook, stirring constantly, until the onions are softened and translucent, about 3 minutes. Add the celery and green pepper and cook until softened, about 5 minutes. Add the garlic and the bay leaves and cook until fragrant, about 2 minutes.

Add the Shrimp Stock to the roux and vegetables. Bring the mixture to a boil, and cook until slightly thickened, about 10 minutes.

Add the crawfish and fat and cook until heated through, about 10 minutes. Add salt and cayenne to taste. Add the butter and stir until melted. Stir in the parsley and green onions. Cook until heated through, another 1-2 minutes. Serve over rice. Garnish with parsley.

(Photograph by Sam Hanna)

Crawfish Florentine

With coral-hued crawfish tails studding the rich, green Florentine sauce, this dish is as beautiful as it is delicious.

Serves 6

½ cup butter
1 large onion, finely chopped
2 lb. peeled and deveined crawfish with their fat (may substitute Gulf shrimp)
½ cup flour
1 cup Shrimp Stock (see index)
4 cups heavy cream
1½ cups fresh spinach, chopped
1 tsp. cayenne pepper
Salt and white pepper
Florentine Rice (recipe follows)

Melt the butter in a 3-qt. saucepan set over medium-high heat. Add the onions and sauté until translucent, about 4 minutes. Add the crawfish (or shrimp), stirring constantly until they begin to color, about 5 minutes. Remove the crawfish (or shrimp) with a slotted spoon and reserve.

To the same pan add the flour and stir until incorporated. Add the stock. Bring to a boil, then reduce to a simmer and cook until thickened, about 4 minutes. Add the cream, increase heat to medium, and cook until thickened, about 10 minutes, taking care never to boil the mixture. Add the reserved crawfish or shrimp and the spinach. Season with cayenne and salt and white pepper to taste. Cook until heated through, about 2 minutes.

Serve over Florentine Rice.

Florentine Rice

This simple, verdant rice pilaf lends a light, bright flavor to any grilled or smothered meat or seafood.

Serves 6

4 tbsp. (½ stick) salted butter
1 medium onion, finely chopped
1 10-oz. bag fresh spinach, rinsed several times, dried, and finely chopped
3 cups hot cooked rice
Salt and pepper

Melt the butter in a skillet over medium-high heat. Add the onion and cook until translucent, about 4 minutes. Add the spinach and cook until wilted and the water released by the spinach has evaporated, about 5 minutes. Add the rice, stir until thoroughly incorporated, and season with salt and pepper to taste.

Crabmeat with Wild Mushrooms and Gnocchi

It's likely that neither Mesdames Bégué nor Castet ever tasted—much less prepared—gnocchi. The airy, doughy pillows hail from Northern Italy and were largely unknown in New Orleans, where Italian immigrants were predominantly Sicilian, until the late twentieth century. This elegant preparation of fresh Gulf crab and wild mushrooms is a favorite from Mark Latter's menu update of 2013.

Serves 6

1 tbsp. extra-virgin olive oil
2 tbsp. unsalted butter
1 lb. mixed wild mushrooms, stemmed if necessary and
    thickly sliced (5 cups)
1 shallot, minced
¼ cup heavy cream
½ tsp. minced fresh thyme
Salt and pepper
1 lb. jumbo lump Gulf crabmeat, picked over
1 lb. fresh, frozen, or dried gnocchi
4 tbsp. freshly grated Parmesan cheese, divided
1 tsp. white truffle oil (optional)

In a large ovenproof skillet, heat the olive oil with the butter over high heat. Add the mushrooms and shallot and cook, stirring occasionally, until browned, about 12 minutes. Reduce the heat to medium and add the cream and thyme. Season with salt and pepper to taste. Bring to a simmer and cook until slightly thickened. Remove from heat and gently stir in the crabmeat. Cover and set aside.

Preheat a low broiler.

Meanwhile, in a large pot of boiling salted water, cook the gnocchi until they float to the surface. Drain and add the gnocchi to the mushroom and crab mixture. Set the skillet over medium heat and return to a gentle simmer. Stir in 2 tbsp. Parmesan, and sprinkle the remaining 2 tbsp. atop mixture.

Broil the mixture 6 inches from the heat until golden and bubbling, about 2-3 minutes. Drizzle with truffle oil if desired.

Shrimp Creole with Grit Cakes

Since Tujague's earliest days, Shrimp Creole has been a regular offering at the restaurant. When Mark Latter took over the reins in 2013, it became a daily part of the menu, year round. He updated the Creole classic with "Grit Cake," with the Southern breakfast staple, grits, serving as a sort of polenta cake.

Serves 6 to 8

½ cup vegetable oil
1 large onion, finely chopped
1 green bell pepper, finely chopped
2 ribs celery, finely shopped
4 large, ripe tomatoes, preferably Creole, peeled,
    seeded, and chopped
½ tsp. cayenne pepper
½ tsp. white pepper
½ tsp. dried basil
1 tsp. dried thyme
2 bay leaves
1 qt. Shrimp Stock (see index)
Salt
2 lb. peeled and deveined Gulf shrimp
½ cup chopped parsley
½ cup chopped green onions
Grit Cakes (recipe follows)

Heat the oil in a heavy pot or Dutch oven, preferably cast iron, set over medium-high heat. Add the onions, bell peppers, and celery and sauté until vegetables are soft and translucent, about 10 minutes. Stir in the tomatoes, cayenne and white pepper, basil, thyme, bay leaves, and Shrimp Stock and return to a boil. Reduce the heat to low and simmer until ingredients break down and sauce thickens slightly, about 1 hour, stirring occasionally. Add salt to taste. Add the shrimp, parsley, and green onions and cook until the shrimp are firm and pink, about 7 minutes. Serve over Grit Cakes.

Grit Cakes

Makes about 12

3 cups cooked grits
½ tsp. granulated garlic
½ cup finely shredded Parmesan cheese
Salt
2 eggs, beaten
2 cups all-purpose flour
Vegetable oil for frying

Blend the grits with the garlic, Parmesan, and salt to taste. Pour the grits onto a sheet pan, spreading evenly. Cool and cut into wedges.

Add the beaten eggs to a bowl. Add the flour to a plate or shallow container. Add enough oil to coat the bottom of a large, preferably nonstick, skillet set over medium-high heat.

Dredge both sides of each grit cake first in the egg, then in the flour. Working in batches if necessary, pan-fry the cakes until golden, about 2 minutes per side. Drain on paper towels and keep warm until serving.

Sautéed Shrimp and Okra with Smoked Sausage

Many people have a prejudice against okra because of the slime. The mucilage, which comes from sugar residues and glycoproteins, can be eliminated through sautéing (or roasting). As you pan-fry the okra, you'll see the slime cooking out, accumulating on the bottom of the pan. A dash of vinegar will also help cut the slime. This old-fashioned favorite can serve as a side or main dish.

Serves 6

1 tbsp. vegetable oil
2 cups okra, trimmed, sliced into ⅛-inch rounds
Creole seasoning
¼ tsp. distilled white vinegar
1 lb. smoked sausage, sliced into ¼-inch rounds
½ cup finely chopped onion
½ cup finely chopped green bell pepper
2 bay leaves
1 tbsp. minced garlic
1 lb. large, raw, peeled, and deveined Gulf shrimp
Hot cooked rice
Parsley leaves for garnish

Add the oil to a skillet set over high heat. Add the okra and season with Creole seasoning to taste. Stir the okra as it cooks. When it takes on a slimy texture, add the vinegar and stir until all of the slime has disappeared, about 1 minute.

Add the sausage and continue cooking. When the okra becomes soft and the fat begins to render from the sausage, add the onion, bell pepper, and bay leaves and cook until the onion is translucent, about 3 minutes. Add the garlic and cook until fragrant, 1 minute more.

Add the shrimp and cook until firm and pink, about 4 minutes. Serve over hot cooked rice. Garnish with parsley leaves.

(Photograph by Sam Hanna)

(Photograph by Sam Hanna)

Trout Meunière Amandine

Meunière *is French for* miller's wife *and here refers to the dusting of flour the trout receives before being lightly sautéed. A Creole standard in New Orleans homes and restaurants, this dish is a century-old favorite at Tujague's.*

Serves 6

1½ cups sliced almonds
6 7- to 8-oz. speckled trout filets, cleaned and boned
Salt and freshly ground black pepper
3 cups all-purpose flour
3 tbsp. vegetable oil
Sauce Meunière, warm (see index)
3 medium lemons, cut into wedges

Preheat the oven to 300 degrees.

Place the almonds in a pan and toast them until golden, about 15-20 minutes, stirring every 5 minutes. Remove from the heat and set aside.

Season the trout filets with salt and pepper and dust with flour. Heat the oil in a large skillet over medium-high heat until the oil shimmers. Working in batches if necessary, add the trout and pan-fry, turning once, until the fish flakes easily with a fork, about 4-5 minutes in all.

Divide the trout filets atop 6 dinner plates. Top each fried trout filet with warm Sauce Meunière and toasted almonds. Garnish with lemon wedges and serve at once.

NOTE: Test the readiness of oil by sprinkling a pinch of flour over it. The flour will brown instantly when the oil is the correct temperature.

Andouille-Crusted Drum with Brown-Butter Vinaigrette

There are two kinds of drum fish—red and black, both plentiful in Louisiana waters. Their flavor and texture are very similar, but any thick, white fish filet can be used in this preparation.

Serves 6

1 lb. andouille sausage, casing removed, sausage
    chopped into ¼-inch pieces
2 cups plain, dry breadcrumbs
2 large eggs
1 cup whole milk
2 cups all-purpose flour
6 7- to 8-oz. drum filets, cleaned, skinned, and boned
Vegetable oil for pan-frying
Brown-Butter Vinaigrette (recipe follows)

Preheat the oven to 350 degrees.

Scatter the andouille on a baking sheet. Place in oven and cook until the fat has completely rendered out, about 15 minutes. Remove the pan from the oven and drain the fat from the andouille. Return the pan to the oven and continue cooking until the andouille is dry and hard, about 15 minutes more. Cool.

Place the andouille and the breadcrumbs in a food processor. Grind the andouille and the breadcrumbs into a powder. Scrape into a shallow plate. Set aside.

Whisk the eggs and milk in a bowl. Add the flour to a separate shallow plate. Dust the drum filets in flour, submerge them in the egg wash, then put them into the andouille and breadcrumb mixture, turning to coat thoroughly.

Add enough vegetable oil to coat the bottom of a large skillet, preferably cast iron, set over medium-high heat. Working in batches if necessary, pan-fry the filets in the hot oil until they have formed a golden crust, about 4 minutes, turning halfway through. Remove the fish to a platter lined with paper towels to drain.

Serve each filet with Brown-Butter Vinaigrette.

Brown-Butter Vinaigrette

Makes 2 cups

1 lb. (4 sticks) salted butter
1 tbsp. fresh lemon juice
1 tbsp. cane vinegar
Black pepper
1 tbsp. chopped fresh parsley

Melt the butter in a medium saucepan over medium heat, whisking constantly for 8-10 minutes until the milk fats begin to brown and the liquid becomes a deep golden color.

Remove the pan from the heat and continue to whisk slowly, adding the lemon juice and the vinegar to the browned butter. The sauce will froth until the acids have evaporated. When the frothing subsides, add pepper to taste. Stir in the parsley.

Chapter 6

And On the Side . . .

(Photograph by Sam Hanna)

Many generations of New Orleanians celebrate Thanksgiving and Christmas with a traditional turkey dinner at Tujague's. Two of those regulars, Elliott and Mary Ann LaBorde, often made the trip from Monroe before retiring to New Orleans. "The waiters make you feel so comfortable, it's like you're dining at home or at Grandma's," they said.

When reminiscing about holidays at Tujague's, Steven Latter commented, "We're different on those days. It's like family. We don't get many kids here usually, but on Thanksgiving and Christmas we get lots of kids and I always try to do something special for them. My own kids are here, too." So strong was Steven's conviction that the only way to learn the restaurant business was from the ground up that he pressed Mark and Mark's future wife, Candace, into kitchen service, where they served the holiday meal together to hundreds of Tujague's patrons.

Mark has his own memories of those holidays. "Holidays? We had no holidays! Thanksgiving and Christmas just meant work! We'd celebrate our Thanksgiving at home the Tuesday before. Then, on Thanksgiving Day, Mom answered the phones. My sister, Shane, worked upstairs as a hostess, seating people and keeping an eye on things, and I originally worked as a busboy."

Shane still loves greeting multiple generations of holiday guests in the second-floor dining rooms. "It's so much fun to watch the babies grow up here over the years."

Aside from the large second-floor room, there are three small dining rooms available for more private gatherings. The LaBordes chuckle over the memory of the year their family numbered ten for Christmas dinner. Steven exclaimed, "Ten? We'll have to put you in a private room because you all are going to be too rowdy!"

Thanksgiving and Christmas may have been working holidays for the Latter family, but they made up for it during Mardi Gras, when the entire second floor was reserved for family and friends. By the time Mark was in college at the University of Alabama, he would delight in bringing friends home for Carnival. "I'd really feel like the big man on campus, with free food and drinks for everyone!"

Special occasions of all kinds have been celebrated at Tujague's. Steven befriended a French Quarter eccentric who was so fond of his dog, he asked if he could throw a birthday party for the mutt at the restaurant. The small upstairs room with the large round table at the center has since been known as Dog Room.

The largest private dining room on Tujague's second floor is the official Krewe d'Etat room. The highly satirical secret Carnival krewe was formed in 1996. New Orleans' old-line Mardi Gras krewes such as Rex, Hermes, Twelfth Night, and Proteus all have their own special dining rooms at Antoine's Restaurant. Originally, Krewe d'Etat would gather in Antoine's Proteus Room but eventually decided they wanted a room of their own. Many original members of Krewe d'Etat were longtime personal friends of Steven Latter. They asked him if they could have a room at Tujague's dedicated to their krewe and he agreed.

The Krewe d'Etat Room is decorated with framed memorabilia such as proclamations from the Dictator, the ruler of this irreverent, rollicking Carnival krewe. A lighted case displays krewe ball favors and special Mardi Gras throws. Their annual celebration at Tujague's is a raucous event where anything goes.

An added feature of the upstairs dining rooms are original floor-to-ceiling French doors that open onto a wide balcony wrapping the corner, from Decatur to Madison. Weather permitting, the doors are opened, allowing parties to move back and forth from dining room to balcony. The view from there is one of the best of New Orleans' French Quarter. Across Decatur stretches the original French Market. To the right are the skyscrapers of the Central Business District. To the left, the gleaming, gold statue of Joan of Arc, triumphantly astride her horse, dominates a small triangular median where Decatur Street splits in two.

Mardi Gras, St. Patrick's Day, St. Joseph's Day, Easter Sunday, even Thanksgiving—New Orleanians are always looking for a reason to parade. There's no better spot than Tujague's balcony to see the parade passing by.

Squash Eldin

When Steven Latter became the proprietor at Tujague's, Eldin Remble was one of the cooks who helped him learn his way around the menu. Eldin acquired his talent for Creole cooking from his mother and grandmother. When Bon Appétit *magazine asked Tujague's for a recipe, they sent Eldin's signature dish.*

Serves 6

6 tbsp. butter
½ onion, finely chopped
1½ lb. fresh yellow squash, sliced
¼ tsp. sugar
¼ tsp. salt
¼ tsp. white pepper
¼ cup Chicken Stock (see index)
1½ tbsp. sweet pimentos, diced

Melt the butter in a skillet over medium-high heat.

Add the onion and sauté until translucent, about 3 minutes.

Add the squash and sprinkle with sugar, salt, and white pepper. Stir to combine. Add the Chicken Stock. Bring to a simmer, cover, reduce heat to medium low, and cook till squash is tender, about 10 minutes.

Stir in the sweet pimentos and serve.

Eldin Remble (Tujague's Private Collection)

Miss Brenda's Creole Oyster Dressing

No Southern holiday table is complete without oyster dressing. It is simply a must *have. For decades, the many families who celebrate their holidays at Tujague's have savored Miss Brenda's version.*

Serves 6

20 small Gulf oysters in their liquor (about ½ lb.)
1 cup cold water
1 stick softened unsalted butter plus 2 tbsp., divided
1½ cups chopped onions
1 cup chopped celery
1 cup chopped bell peppers
¼ tsp. dried oregano leaves
¼ tsp. dried thyme leaves
1 tsp. minced garlic
3 bay leaves
1 cup fine, dry breadcrumbs
Creole seasoning
¼ cup chopped green onions

Combine oysters and water; stir and refrigerate for at least 1 hour. Strain and reserve oysters and oyster water separately in refrigerator until ready to use.

Preheat oven to 350 degrees.

Melt 1 stick butter in a large skillet, preferably cast iron, over high heat. Add the onions, celery, and bell pepper; sauté until onions are dark brown but not burned, about 8 minutes, stirring frequently.

Add the oregano, thyme, garlic, and bay leaves. Reduce heat to medium and cook until fragrant, about 1 minute.

Stir in the reserved oyster water, increase heat to high, and cook until some of the liquid has evaporated, about 10 minutes, stirring occasionally.

Add enough breadcrumbs to make a moist but not runny dressing. Add Creole seasoning to taste.

Remove from heat. Stir in drained oysters. Spoon dressing into an ungreased 8x8x2-inch baking dish and bake, uncovered, until golden and bubbling. Remove from oven, and stir in 2 tbsp. butter and green onions. Remove and discard bay leaves.

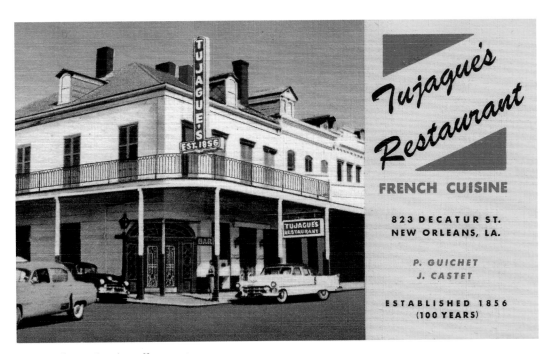

(From the author's collection)

Miss Brenda's Cornbread Dressing

While oyster dressing is regarded as holiday fare, any day is just right for rich, buttery, easy-to-make cornbread dressing. It is especially wonderful when served with a thick, juicy pork chop.

Serves 8 to 10

Miss Brenda's Cornbread (see index)
1½ cups soft breadcrumbs
1 stick butter
1 medium onion, diced
3 ribs celery, diced
2 tbsp. finely chopped fresh thyme or 1 tbsp. dried
4 cups Chicken Stock (see index), or use store-bought
Black pepper

Grease a 13x9-inch baking dish.

Crumble the cornbread into a large bowl, stir in breadcrumbs, and set aside.

Melt the butter in a large skillet over medium heat. Add the onions and celery and sauté until tender, about 5 minutes. Stir in the thyme and sauté until fragrant, about 1 more minute.

Stir the vegetables into the reserved cornbread. Add Chicken Stock (use more or less to achieve desired texture) and pepper to taste; pour evenly into the baking dish. Cover and chill 8 hours.

Preheat oven to 375 degrees. Bake the casserole, uncovered, until golden, about 40 minutes.

(Tujague's Private Collection)

(Photograph by Sam Hanna)

Madame Bégué's Eggplant with Rice and Ham

Much like a jambalaya, this recipe is a creation of Madame Bégué. To transform it into a substantial entrée, substitute shrimp stock for the water called for here and toss in a half-pound of raw, peeled shrimp during the last 5 minutes of the cooking process.

Serves 4 to 6

6 tbsp. butter
½ cup diced ham
1 onion, chopped
1 eggplant, peeled and cut into ¼-inch cubes
1 cup long-grain white rice
2 cups water
½ tsp. dried thyme leaves
2 bay leaves
Salt and black pepper

Melt the butter in a 3½-qt. heavy saucepan set over medium-high heat. Add the ham and sauté until browned, about 5 minutes. Add the onion and sauté until translucent, about 4 minutes more.

Add the eggplant and sauté until softened, about 10 minutes. Add the rice and stir well to combine. Add the water, thyme, and bay leaves. Bring to a boil, cover, and reduce heat to low. Cook undisturbed for 25 minutes.

Stir well and, if necessary, add more water, cover, and cook for an additional 5-10 minutes until rice is fully cooked. Add salt and pepper to taste.

Miss Brenda's Spinach Casserole

This is quick and easy yet special enough for the holiday sideboard.

Serves 6

3 10-oz. pkg. frozen spinach
8 oz. cream cheese, softened
½ cup melted butter, divided
1 cup seasoned breadcrumbs
Paprika (optional)

Preheat oven to 350 degrees.

Thaw spinach and press or squeeze to remove excess water. Grease a casserole dish and set aside.

In a large mixing bowl, combine the spinach, cream cheese, and ¼ cup melted butter. Spoon into casserole dish. Sprinkle with the breadcrumbs and paprika, if desired, and drizzle with remaining ¼ cup butter. Bake for 25 minutes.

Opposite: *Everyone's favorite watering hole* (Tujague's Private Collection)

Just another day at Tujague's (Photograph by Louis Sahuc)

Chapter 7

Just Desserts: The Second Madame's Ambition

Françoise Laforgue Laporte was a widow with a young son when Hipolyte and Elizabeth Bégué welcomed her into their kitchen at the acclaimed Bégué's Exchange. When Hipolyte's older wife, the celebrated "Creole *cuisinière*" Elizabeth, died in October of 1906, he closed the restaurant for one day and then reopened with Françoise, the former assistant, in charge of Madame's kitchen. In May 1908, Hipolyte married Françoise, formally making her the second Madame.

Although she continued to cook Elizabeth's famous dishes, Françoise made changes at the historic establishment. Competing with other successful restaurants of the day, she added a six o'clock dinner service to the long-established eleven o'clock brunch, thus doubling her daily clientele.

When the owner of the building at Madison and Decatur significantly raised the rent in 1915, the ambitious second Madame bought a larger building on the opposite side of Madison. Before the move could take place, on September 20, 1915, a hurricane tore the roof off of the new building, delaying the move and requiring further output of funds.

Finally, on August 8, 1916, the Bégués move was reported in the *Times-Picayune.* "Her son, Emile Laporte, waiters and Madame's entire household of retainers moved with the restaurant, as did the faithful old coterie of epicures, who would follow Madame to the ends of the earth and probably starve if she forsook them. In her new building, Madame can now serve 150 guests."

She advertised in the *States Item:*

Madame Begue, established forty years. Same old stand, Madison and Decatur. For ladies and gentlemen. Breakfast 11 a.m. $1.50, Table d'hote 6 p.m. 75 cents. Cuisine Unexcelled.

Françoise Laforgue Laporte Bégué in Bégué's kitchen
(The Historic New Orleans Collection, acc. no. 1981.261.32)

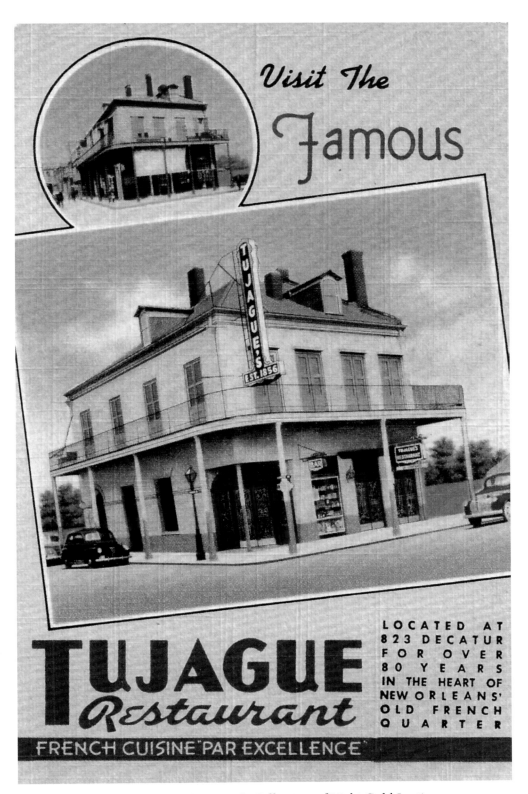

A 1946 Tujague's postcard (Collection of Vicki Gold Levi)

Hipolyte Bégué wearing Loving Cup (The Historic New Orleans Collection, acc. no. 1981.261.34)

But instead of the anticipated financial success, the new restaurant brought nothing but grief to Françoise. About a month after the move, on September 14, she again made the news, when the *Daily States* reported: "The left arm of Madame Begue, famous cook, was fractured Tuesday night by a dumb waiter in her restaurant on Decatur Street. Madame Begue, in the kitchen on the second floor was placing dishes on the dumb waiter to send them to the dining room below when the dumb waiter descended suddenly and snapped her arm."

Into his old age, Hipolyte remained a constant presence in the restaurant's dining rooms, always acting the affable host in the style of a nineteenth-century bon vivant, even as his health declined.

On May 14, 1916, the local papers reported:

> For the first time in many years, Hipolyte Begue, the famous restaurateur did not preside at his own dinner table. Friday night patrons of the quaint café near the French Market wondered what had become of him. Their concern at his absence was unexpectedly relieved by a late diner.
>
> It seems Monsieur Begue, who has been suffering for years from rheumatic gout, was greatly relieved by the recent warm weather and displayed an ambition to take a short trip beyond the vicinity of his café. At the same time, Joe Mandot appeared in his automobile and joyfully announced the capture of 2 large stingrays. If Monsieur Begue had any doubt as to the wisdom of taking the trip, they were dissipated by this news.
>
> With the New Orleans crack lightweight, Monsieur Begue motored to the Mandot camp at Milneburg where a large number of the boxer's friends had assembled. The stingrays were produced and Monsieur Begue prepared them in a way all his own. Ordinarily, no one would eat this kind of fish, but those in the party are authority for the statement that the dish was delicious.

> Monsieur Begue was asked later to explain his method of preparing the fish. He said they must first be boiled, then smothered under Bordelaise and finally finished with "black butter" sauce. But it's a safe bet that even with these instructions the average cook could not produce the result shown by the aged restaurateur.

The restaurant's expansion proved too much for Françoise's aging husband. On April 5, 1917, Hipolyte died at the age of seventy-eight from a "stroke of paralysis." In an act of revisionist history, Françoise claimed in Hipolyte's obituary that he had come to New Orleans at the age of sixteen to work for his uncle in the butcher's market. "He saved money to open a saloon and restaurant known as Begue's Exchange."

There was no mention of the first Madame, Elizabeth, who had opened the original "Exchange" with her first husband, Louis Dutrey, long before Hipolyte appeared on the scene and whose recipes were still responsible for the restaurant's success. In Hipolyte's obituary, Françoise further embellished her role by saying:

With the advent of the second Madame, business was extended to include a dinner at 6 p.m.

For the past several years his intellect was fading and he had no active part in the business. Madame did the marketing and supervised the cooking and service with her son Emile Laporte.

So began Françoise's long steady decline. By the spring of 1918, she was in bankruptcy and her new building and its contents were sold at auction. Trying to make the best of it, she announced in the newspaper that Bégué's was moving to the upstairs rooms of the Old Absinthe House on Bourbon Street. There is no evidence that she ever made that move.

Instead, Françoise annually registered the business with the city at varying addresses throughout the 1920s and early '30s—504 Madison and 504 St. Ann among them.

A 1928 newspaper article focused on the deplorable condition of the lower Pontalba, describing the location as "a rodent infested cesspool." It stated, "Finally, the only tenant of the lower Pontalba was Madame Begue."

Throughout the years, Emile worked in the restaurant business with his mother, assuming the hosting role of his stepfather, Hipolyte Bégué. After Françoise's death in 1935, Emile continued to trade on the faded Bégué glory, with his wife, Katie, playing the part of Madame.

In 1938, the *WPA New Orleans City Guide* lists Bégué's at 504 Madison, with Katie Laporte as proprietor. It states:

> The market restaurant, located originally at 207 Decatur Street, lives today chiefly in its past. This restaurant, flourishing in the "gay nineties" was famous for its Bohemian breakfasts, six-course affairs lasting from 11 o'clock to 2 or 3 p.m. The present restaurant is situated upstairs over a corner garage in the rooms where Hypolite Begue had his latter-day restaurant.

Emile Laporte closed Bégué's in 1941 and, in a strange turn of events, worked briefly as bar manager at Tujague's. In 1944, at the age of forty-seven, he died of a stroke. Emile's last job before his death was as a bartender at Pat O'Brien's.

Curiously, at approximately the same time, today's great Creole *cuisinière,* Leah Chase, was working at her first job. At the age of seventeen, she worked as a waitress at the Old Coffee Pot restaurant, next door to Pat O'Brien's. "There was a woman who came in every day, dressed all in black. We used to call her 'The Widow Bégué,'" Leah recalled. "She was a cleaning lady at Pat O'Brien's, I think. I wonder who she was?"

Who was "The Widow Bégué"? Perhaps Emile Laporte's widow, Katie?

That answer is lost in the mists of time but makes for great lore—especially when served with a side of just desserts.

Established 1856
Visit the Famous
TUJAGUE RESTAURANT
French Cuisine Par Excellence
Table D'Hote Daily
Lunch: 11 A.M. to 3 P.M.
Dinner: 5 P.M. to 9 P.M.
Sunday: 11 A.M. to 9 P.M.
Closed on Friday
Tele.: 523-9462 - 823 DECATUR ST.
NEW ORLEANS, LA.

Purse-size mirror produced for Tujague's centennial (Tujague's Private Collection)

TUJAGUE'S
1856 - 1986

Souvenir purse-size mirror commemorating the restaurant's 130th anniversary
(Tujague's Private Collection)

(Photograph by Sam Hanna)

Grasshopper Pie

This creamy, minty delight does justice to its namesake, the famous Grasshopper cocktail.

Serves 6 to 8

½ tbsp. granulated gelatin (such as Knox)
2 tbsp. crème de menthe (green or clear)
2 tbsp. clear crème de cacao
1 qt. plus 1 cup heavy cream, divided
1½ cups finely chopped white chocolate, divided
¼ cup mini marshmallows
Green food coloring
½ tbsp. cream of tartar
¼ cup powdered sugar
½ cup finely chopped milk chocolate
Oreo Cookie Crust (recipe follows)

Combine the gelatin, crème de menthe, and crème de cacao. Set aside until the gelatin blooms, about 5 minutes.

Scald 1 cup heavy cream. Add the gelatin mixture and stir to combine.

Combine 1 cup chopped white chocolate and the marshmallows in a food processor and pulse to combine, about 1 minute. With the processor running, stream in the hot gelatin and cream mixture. Add green food coloring to achieve desired color (the mixture will lighten by 50 percent when it is later folded into whipped cream). Scrape the mixture into a stainless-steel bowl and refrigerate, stirring every 5 minutes until chilled, about 30 minutes.

Pour the remaining 1 qt. cream into a large, chilled, stainless-steel bowl. Add the cream of tartar and powdered sugar and whisk until stiff peaks form, about 8 minutes. Scrape half of the whipped cream into another bowl. Slowly fold in the refrigerated cream and gelatin mixture. Fold in the remaining whipped cream. Finally, fold in the remaining chopped white and the milk chocolate. Scrape into the Oreo Cookie Crust. Chill for 4 hours.

Oreo Cookie Crust

Makes 1 9-inch piecrust

20 Oreo cookies
3 tbsp. unsalted butter, melted

Finely grind cookies in a food processor. Add the melted butter and blend until moist crumbs form. Press the crumb mixture onto bottom and up sides of 9-inch-diameter metal spring-form pan. Freeze the crust until firm, about 10 minutes.

Classic Bread Pudding with Holiday Cranberry Sauce

With its bracing, ruby-hued sauce, this rich pudding is an ideal make-ahead dessert for the holiday feast.

Serves 8 to 10

2 loaves stale French bread, cut into 1-inch-thick slices
3 sticks butter, melted
4 cups sugar
¼ cup vanilla
Pinch of nutmeg
15 eggs, beaten
1 pt. orange juice
¼ cup brandy
4 cups milk
¼ cup raisins
Holiday Cranberry Sauce (recipe follows)

Grease an 8x10-inch baking dish and press the bread rounds into the bottom.

In a large mixing bowl, combine the melted butter, sugar, vanilla, nutmeg, eggs, orange juice, brandy, and milk. Pour the mixture over the bread and allow to soak for at least 15 minutes, preferably overnight, pressing down on the bread occasionally.

Preheat the oven to 350 degrees.

Sprinkle the raisins atop the bread pudding and bake until golden and puffed, about 45 minutes.

Holiday Cranberry Sauce

Makes about 2½ cups

1 14-oz. can whole-berry cranberry sauce
2 tsp. vanilla
¼ cup brandy
1 cup sugar
4 tbsp. butter, divided
5 tbsp. cornstarch dissolved in 7 oz. water (a slurry)

Combine the cranberry sauce, vanilla, brandy, sugar, and 2 tbsp. butter in a 1½-qt. saucepot. Bring to a boil. Slowly whisk the slurry into the cranberry mixture until a thick, creamy consistency is achieved. Remove from the heat and whisk in the remaining butter. Serve immediately on hot bread pudding.

Tujague's Pecan Pie

In 1986, Steven Latter seized the opportunity to promote his new business by celebrating the 130th anniversary of Tujague's Restaurant. Throughout the fall of that year, he held various events designed to bring attention to the special anniversary. He dedicated one of the private dining rooms to former governor James A. Noe and began serving a new appetizer named for him, Oysters à la Governor Noe. New Orleans mayor Sidney Barthelemy proclaimed November to be Tujague's Month, *celebrated in grand style at a special luncheon on Saturday, November 1, 1986. A dessert contest was held to determine whose recipe deserved the designation of "bon temps pecan pie." The judges were New Orleans' top chefs of the day, Warren LeRuth, Paul Prudhomme, and Willy Coln. New Orleans resident Joanne Champagne was declared the winner and her pecan pie recipe joined bread pudding on the restaurant's menu.*

Serves 6 to 8

Butter Piecrust (recipe follows)
3 eggs
1 cup sugar
⅔ cup dark corn syrup
2 tbsp. butter, melted
1 tsp. vanilla
⅛ tsp. salt
3 tbsp. bourbon
1 ½ cups pecan halves

Preheat the oven to 400 degrees.

Make the Butter Piecrust and set aside.

In a mixing bowl, beat the eggs. Blend in the sugar, corn syrup, melted butter, vanilla, and salt. Stir in the bourbon and pecan halves. Pour the mixture into the piecrust and bake for 10 minutes. Reduce the heat to 350 degrees and continue baking until the filling is set and the crust is browned, about 30 minutes or more. Cool on a wire rack before serving.

Butter Piecrust

Makes 1 9-inch piecrust

1 cup all-purpose flour
1 tsp. sugar
½ tsp. salt
⅓ cup shortening
1 tbsp. chilled butter
2 tbsp. cold water

In a bowl, mix together the flour, sugar, and salt. Blend in the shortening and the chilled butter with a pastry cutter until they are thoroughly combined. The mixture should be crumbly. Pour in the cold water and blend well to bind the dough.

Shape the dough into a ball. Place on a flat, lightly floured surface and roll it out with a lightly floured rolling pin. The dough should extend 2 inches beyond the 9-inch pie pan. Fit the dough in the pie pan and crimp the edges.

(Photograph by Sam Hanna)

Index